Collective Biographies

AMERICAN HORROR WRITERS

Bob Madison

Enslow Publishers, Inc.

40 Industrial Road	PO Box 38
Box 398	Aldershot
Berkeley Heights, NJ 07922	Hants GU12 6BP
USA	UK

http://www.enslow.com

Library of Congress Cataloging-in-Publication Data

Madison, Bob.
    American horror writers / Bob Madison.
        p. cm. — (Collective biographies)
    Includes bibliographical references and index.
    Contents: Edgar Allan Poe — Ambrose Bierce — H.P. Lovecraft — Robert
Bloch — Shirley Jackson — Rod Serling — Dean Koontz — R.L. Stine — Anne
Rice — Stephen King.
    ISBN 0-7660-1379-0
    1. Horror tales, American—History and criticism Juvenile literature.
    2. Authors, American—20th century—Biography Juvenile literature.
    3. Authors, American—19th century—Biography Juvenile literature.
    [1. Authors, American. 2. Horror stories—History and criticism.]
    I. Title. II. Series.
    PS374.H67M33 2000
    813'.0873809—dc21
                                  99-41494
                                    CIP

To Our Readers:
All Internet Addresses in this book were active and appropriate when we went to press.
Any comments or suggestions can be sent by e-mail to Comments@enslow.com or to
the address on the back cover.

Illustration Credits: AP/World Wide Photos, p. 82; ©1991 Beth Gwinn,
p. 32; ©Carroll S. Grevemberg, p. 74; Courtesy of Bantam Books, Photo
©Jerry Bauer, p. 58; Courtesy of Bob Madison, p. 39; Courtesy of Kimberly
Florky, p. 79; Courtesy of Necronomicon Press, pp. 24, 30; Courtesy of
R. L. Stine, p. 70; Courtesy of Rod Serling Memorial Foundation, p. 48;
Courtesy of the Stanley Hotel, p. 90; Enslow Publishers, Inc., p. 63;
Courtesy of Scholastic, Inc., with permission of R. L. Stine, p. 66; Library
of Congress, pp. 8, 15; National Archives, p. 22; Reproduced from the
Dictionary of American Portraits, Published by Dover Publications, Inc., in
1967, p. 18; Syracuse University, Syracuse, New York, pp. 42, 46;
www.scifi.com/twizone/twilight5.html, p54.

Cover Illustration: Edgar Allan Poe, Library of Congress.

Contents

Preface

People like to be scared. Perhaps that is the best way to explain why so many Americans read horror stories and go to horror movies.

Writers have been scaring people for centuries. The earliest horror stories to come out of Europe, such as *Frankenstein* by Mary Shelley, relied upon remote and spooky countryside, local folktales and ancient castles to inspire chills. But, America had no castles or deranged aristocrats. As a result, American authors developed their own style of horror stories. These stories were more natural, set in recognizable places, and had a greater understanding of psychology.

Even the earliest American authors wrote horror stories. In 1820, Washington Irving wrote of the Headless Horseman haunting Ichabod Crane in *The Legend of Sleepy Hollow*. Later, Edgar Allan Poe was the first American writer to gain fame primarily through his scary stories. Writers who followed Poe, such as H. P. Lovecraft, tried to imitate his style. Others, like Robert Bloch and Shirley Jackson, wrote stories set in contemporary America. As you will see, American horror fiction progressed from the fog-bound castles of Europe and quickly found an American voice. In America, horror stories are just as likely to take place in a local hamburger restaurant as in an old dark house.

American authors also pioneered the field of pulp magazines, which helped increase the readership of horror stories. Pulp magazines were cheaply printed magazines containing stories of adventure, mystery, horror, and science fiction. These inexpensive magazines gave many readers their first taste of horror stories and also provided opportunities for new authors to get published. Some of the most popular characters of the past century were first introduced in the pulps, including Tarzan of the Apes, the Shadow, and Conan the Barbarian.

Although each of the ten authors profiled in this book came to horror writing from a different background, all shared a vivid imagination and a dedication to becoming writers. Many of the authors in this book started writing stories during their childhood. But, success for these ten authors came only after years of hard work. All of these authors worked at perfecting the craft of writing and fulfilled their dreams of being writers.

These ten authors are bound together by the force of their imaginations and the ability to tell good stories. The ghouls and goblins they have created may be make-believe, but the commitment, hard work, and dedication they all share has been very real.

When you read the short stories and novels mentioned in this book, use what you know about the author to bring insight into what they have written. Remember the sadness of Poe, Lovecraft's affection for New England and Rice's tragic loss of her daughter. A greater familiarity with these authors' lives will help you to enjoy their stories all the more.

Scary stories have been around for thousands of years, and will be around for thousands more. The most special thing about this type of story is the fun of being frightened by make-believe. As long as people enjoy worlds of the imagination, there will always be a place for scary stories.

Edgar Allan Poe

Edgar Allan Poe
(1809–1849)

Edgar Allan Poe was born in Boston, on January 19, 1809. Edgar's parents, David and Elizabeth Poe, were both actors. When Poe was one year old, his alcoholic father vanished, leaving Elizabeth to care for Edgar, his older brother William, and the youngest sister, Rosalie, who was mentally handicapped.

After David Poe left the family, Elizabeth continued her stage career and tried to raise her family as best she could. They moved from town to town, and in Richmond, Virginia, Elizabeth's chronic cough turned into a seizure that later killed her. Edgar Allan Poe was only two years old when he watched his mother die of tuberculosis. Like a scene from one of his stories, Edgar sat in a boarding house beside his mother, watching her cough up blood as tuberculosis destroyed her lungs.[1]

After his mother died, Edgar was taken into the home of John Allan, a wealthy cotton merchant. Allan became Edgar Allan Poe's godfather, but never formally adopted him. Though there were periods of warmth between the two, John Allan and Edgar often quarreled bitterly.

In 1815, John Allan took his family to England, hoping to expand his cotton business. Within five years, John Allan's business soured and the family returned to Richmond. In Richmond, Edgar received good grades in school.

In 1826, at the age of seventeen, Edgar Allan Poe went to the University of Virginia in Charlottesville. Poe only spent one year at the university, but started writing many poems and developed a love for writing. While Poe was at school, John Allan refused to give him any money. Poe tried gambling at cards to raise cash, but lost heavily. Eventually the gambling debts forced Poe to leave the university.

It was also at the university that Poe first started to drink. Poe drank while he gambled, and he also got drunk easily. Many people who have studied Poe's life believe that he was allergic to alcohol, and that even little amounts of alcohol had a terrible effect on him.[2]

During this period, Edgar Allan Poe had a difficult time deciding what to do with his life. When he returned to Richmond, John Allan put Poe to work without pay as a bookkeeper in the family business. Poe only stayed in Richmond for three months before he ran away in March 1827. Moving to Boston, Poe printed a small volume of poems, *Tamerlane*, but he was not able to make much money writing. That year, Poe decided to join the army under the name of Edgar A. Perry. He was sent to Fort Moultrie, on Sullivan's Island, off the coast of Charleston, Virginia. Poe would later use the island as the setting for one of his famous mystery stories, "The Gold-Bug."

Poe quickly found that he hated the orderly life of a soldier, and begged John Allan to get him out of the service. At first Allan refused, but when John Allan's wife, Frances, fell ill, she convinced her husband to have mercy on Poe before she died. John Allan sent for Poe and promised that their relationship would improve if Poe entered the United States Military Academy at West Point.

Poe published another collection of poetry in 1829 before entering West Point in 1830. He easily passed the entrance exam, and spent two months in basic training. Though Poe maintained very high grades, he again found military life too confining. Sensitive, and sometimes wild, Poe disliked the discipline and severe punishments that were common at West Point. Unhappy at West Point, Poe purposely got himself expelled.[3]

Also in 1830, Frances Allan died and John Allan soon remarried. Poe and Allan continued to argue about money in letters they wrote to each other. Allan accused Poe of being ungrateful, while Poe wrote that Allan did not fulfill his financial responsibilities to him. Finally, Allan disowned Poe, leaving the young man all alone in the world.

After West Point, Poe moved to New York and then to Baltimore, where he wrote short stories. Poe wrote several stories for a contest held by the *Philadelphia Saturday Courier* newspaper, but did not win. The stories were published later, and in 1833, Poe won fifty dollars for his story "MS Found in a Bottle." Poe continued writing fiction and began to write for the *Southern Literary Messenger* magazine. He became the magazine's editor in 1835 and jealously attacked other well-known writers in his magazine, making many enemies.

Poe went to live with his aunt, Marie Poe Clemm, whom he called "Mother." Marie Clemm arranged for Poe to marry her daughter, his thirteen year-old cousin Virginia in 1836. Because of their close relation, Poe and Virginia pretended to be brother and sister for the first two years of their marriage. Poe would call his wife "Sis" while they were married, and the both of them lived with Mrs. Clemm.

It was after marrying Virginia that Poe wrote the majority of his most famous stories and poems. He wrote his only book-length story of horror, *The Narrative of A. Gordon Pym*, in 1838, and resigned from the job at the *Messenger*. Edgar Allan Poe,

Virginia, and Marie Clemm moved to Philadelphia, Pennsylvania. Poe began work as a literary editor for *Graham's Magazine* in 1840. He served as a critic and helped bring new readers to the magazine with his stories and reviews.

In 1840, Poe released his first book of short stories, *Tales of the Grotesque and Arabesque*. Though it is now considered a classic, it sold poorly. The book featured one of Poe's most celebrated horror stories, "The Fall of the House of Usher." In that tale, Roderick Usher, believing his family to be contaminated by madness, buries his sister Madeline alive.

In 1841 Poe wrote "The Murders in the Rue Morgue," which is recognized as the first detective story. The tale—about the murder of a young woman—is the first to deal with a private detective and present clues for the reader to solve the crime. Poe wrote two sequels: "The Mystery of Marie Roget" in 1842 and "The Purloined Letter," in 1844.

Poe resigned as editor of *Graham's Magazine* in 1842. He still wrote a few reviews and essays for *Graham's*.

In early 1842, Virginia broke a blood vessel in her throat while singing, and her health began to fail. She became infected with tuberculosis. Poe moved Virginia and Marie Clemm to New York, hoping that treatment in New York would be better for Virginia.

Poe continued to write. "The Tell-Tale Heart," first published in the Boston *Pioneer* in January,

1843, is about a man who becomes obsessed with an older man's vulture-like eye. He kills the man and hides the body before the police come. Another tale, "The Premature Burial," first published in the *Dollar Newspaper* on July 31, 1844, told the story of a man who fears being buried alive.

Poe's fame grew when he published his poem, "The Raven." At the time Poe was working as editor of *Broadway Journal* magazine. Poe also started a series of lectures, touring many eastern cities and reading from his growing body of poems and short stories. Unfortunately, drinking again became a problem for Poe. He frequently arrived at his readings drunk, enraging the audiences.

In early 1847, Poe sat by helplessly as Virginia grew sicker with tuberculosis. Poe had money for neither blankets nor firewood to warm her frail body. Poe felt so guilty about the poverty in which Virginia died that he became ill, too. Marie Clemm helped him recover, but Poe never fully regained his health.[4] During the last two years of his life, Poe wrote many stories and poems. He even tried to revitalize his private life by starting two romances. But Poe's problems with alcohol and unreliability prevented any lasting relationship.

In September 1849, Poe traveled to Baltimore to start fresh. No one really knows what happened, but five days later, on October 3, Poe was found wandering the streets of the city in a daze.[5] He was taken to Washington Hospital, where he died on October 7,

Poe's fame grew when he published his poem, "The Raven." In this illustration for the poem, the raven terrifies the man with its call of "Nevermore."

1849, without ever fully regaining consciousness. He was buried in the Westminster Churchyard.

Before his death, Poe arranged for his writings and papers to be cared for by an editor-writer named Rufus Griswold. Unfortunately for Poe, Griswold wrote an obituary full of lies about Edgar Allan Poe, and spread many rumors about him. Many of the rumors started by Griswold, including stories of drug addiction, continue to this day.[6]

Poe was a brilliant writer of stories and poems. Poe invented the detective story, helped popularize the short story and was the first great practitioner of the scary story in the United States. It is his poetic gifts along with his tales of the "grotesque and arabesque" that are his true legacy.

Ambrose Bierce
(1842–1914?)

Ambrose Gwinnet Bierce was born on June 24, 1842, in Meigs County, Ohio. He was one of thirteen children, all of whom had names that began with the letter A. It was his father, Marcus Aurelius Bierce, who named them all and raised his children under strict Christian principles. Ambrose hated his family and could hardly wait to get away from them.[1]

Ambrose Bierce left home at age fifteen to work as a printer's assistant for the *Northern Indianian* newspaper in Warsaw, Indiana. While working there, a staff member falsely accused him of stealing money and Bierce left the position. Though he no longer lived with his family, his parents insisted that he enroll in the Kentucky Military Institute. At the

Ambrose Bierce

Institute, Ambrose learned tactical thinking and map reading. These skills proved very useful when he enlisted in the Union Army during the Civil War in 1861.[2]

Ambrose Bierce was only nineteen years old when the Civil War began, and by the war's end, he was a deeply cynical man. The war also helped make Bierce a writer. After witnessing the death and despair of the Civil War, Bierce was compelled to put his experiences of war down on paper. Many of his famous ghost stories, including "An Occurrence at Owl Creek Bridge" and "Chickamauga," took place during the Civil War.[3]

After the war Bierce bounced between a number of positions in the federal government. He finally found a position as a night guard at the United States Mint. He read constantly in his spare time and began writing as well. In 1868, Bierce wrote pamphlets that mocked the presidential candidates, which he shared with his co-workers. People who worked for both campaigns discovered the pamphlets and distributed them widely.

Bierce tried writing poetry, but failed. His short stories, however, were popular and he published many of them in such magazines as the *Californian, Alta California, Golden Era,* and *News-Letter and California Advertiser.* He developed his own column for the *News-Letter* and, at age twenty-six, became editor of that newspaper. He stayed until 1872, writing one hundred and sixty-seven weekly columns.

In 1871, Ambrose Bierce married Mary Ellen (Mollie) Day, from one of the best families in San Francisco. Bierce's new father-in-law sent the young couple on a long honeymoon in England as a wedding present. In London, Bierce was accepted into the "Fleet Street Gang," a group of journalists and writers. Bierce wrote for English magazines and newspapers, and published his first book, *The Fiend's Delight,* a year later. Because of Bierce's bitter cynicism and biting wit, he became known as "Bitter Bierce."[4]

The Bierces had two children while in England, Day, born in 1872, and Leigh, born in 1874. Mollie Bierce left England, but Ambrose stayed behind, working on all kinds of projects. One job was editing a magazine called the *Lantern,* which was sponsored by the Empress Eugenie, wife of the former emperor Napoleon III of France. Bierce both edited and wrote most of the articles.

Bierce finally returned to San Francisco and joined his wife and three children: Day, Leigh, and newborn daughter, Helen. He returned to work at the Mint but continued writing stories for magazines and newspapers. Bierce spent 1880 hoping to strike it rich gold mining in the Black Hills of South Dakota while working for Wells Fargo & Co. After returning home, he became editor of a weekly publication, *Wasp.*

In 1887 newspaper publisher William Randolph Hearst asked Bierce to write for his newspaper, the

San Francisco Examiner. Bierce worked there for the next twenty years, mostly writing a column he called "Prattle." While doing the column, Bierce started writing satirical definitions to everyday words. These would be collected in 1906 under the title *The Cynics Word Book*, and revised in 1911 as *The Devil's Dictionary.*

The definitions in *The Devil's Dictionary* reveal Bierce at his wicked best. For example, Bierce defined a *zoo* as "a place where animals from all over the world come to see men, women and children behave like fools."

In 1891 Bierce published his first collection of horror stories, *Tales of Soldiers and Civilians.* It contains many of the tales that have led to his reputation as a great "shadow-maker." *Tales of Soldiers and Civilians* stories included "The Damned Thing," about an invisible entity stalking the wheat fields at night, and "The Middle Toe of the Right Foot," about revenge from beyond the grave. In "The Suitable Surroundings," a writer of horror stories bets his friend that he could not read his story in a deserted house because the reader would die of fright.[5]

While working at the *Examiner,* Bierce attacked "railrogues," executives in the railroad industry. The leading railroads made a great deal of money and tried to get extensions on paying large government loans. One railroad tycoon trying to get a $75 million loan deferment from Washington offered Bierce a bribe. Bierce said: "My price is seventy-five million dollars. If, when you are ready to pay, I happen to be out of town, you may hand it over to my friend, the Treasurer of the United States."[6]

One of the themes of Bierce's stories is the relationships between family members. In the 1893 collection of stories, *Can Such Things Be?*, for example, the story "The Death of Halpin Frayser," is about a man who is haunted by the ghost of his mother. Bierce drew these stories from his own family tragedies. Bierce watched as his son Leigh died of pneumonia brought on by alcoholism, and Day died

Many of Bierce's famous ghost stories, including "An Occurrence at Owl Creek Bridge" and "Chickamauga," took place during the Civil War. These Union soldiers wait in the trenches before a battle near Petersburg, Virginia, in 1865.

due to wounds received in a duel over a woman. He also grew distant from Mollie and had periods of separation from her before she filed for divorce in 1904. She died a year later, before the divorce was finalized.

Bierce retired from the *Examiner* in 1908. Four years later, when he was seventy years old, he visited the places he knew in his younger days, including battlefields of the Civil War. He went to Texas, where he was given a tribute dinner by his old army buddies.

In December, 1913, Ambrose Bierce crossed into war-torn Mexico. His last letter was dated December 26, and came from the small town of Chihuahua. There he vanished, never to be seen again.

Ambrose Bierce is important to the evolution of the American horror story: he used his experience as a journalist to bring a sense of realism to his stories. By putting the horrors of war and man's cruelty to man in a supernatural setting, Ambrose Bierce was able to combine horror and realism. This new approach was key to the development of a distinctive American style of horror literature.

Howard Phillips Lovecraft

H. P. Lovecraft
(1890–1937)

When he was a boy, Howard Phillips Lovecraft would listen to horror stories his grandfather told him. Young Lovecraft liked these stories so much that he decided to write his own. When he was six, Howard wrote "The Noble Eavesdropper," and he continued writing weird tales until his early death, at age forty-seven.[1]

Howard was born on August 20, 1890, in his family home in Providence, Rhode Island. His mother was Sarah Susan Phillips, whose family came to America in 1630. His father, Winfield Scott Lovecraft, was a traveling salesman. Howard was often unhappy and depressed as a youth, so he used his imagination to create worlds where he was more comfortable.

When Howard was three years old, his father had a nervous breakdown in a Chicago hotel and was brought back to a Rhode Island hospital. Winfield Lovecraft stayed in the hospital for five years, and died there in 1898.

Howard was brought up by his mother; his two aunts, Lillian D. Clark and Annie E. Phillips Gamwell; and his grandfather, Whipple Van Buren Phillips. Lovecraft was a frail child who suffered from many illnesses. He attended school irregularly, but he read a great deal on his own. When Howard was eight years old he became interested in science, especially chemistry and astronomy. Howard started to write about these subjects, and published his own work for his schoolmates.

Howard went to Hope Street High School, in Providence. Things had been going well for the Lovecraft family until 1904, when his grandfather Whipple Phillips died. With little money, Howard and his mother left the large house and moved into a small apartment. Howard had loved his old house and was very unhappy moving.

Lovecraft's unhappiness increased and just before he graduated high school, in 1908, he had a nervous breakdown. The breakdown left him in delicate health, so he did not finish school and get his diploma. His sensitive nature also prevented him from going to college.

It took a long time for Lovecraft to recover. He remembered the period between 1908 and 1913 by writing "in those days I could hardly bear to see or speak to anyone, & liked to shut out the world by pulling down dark shades & using artificial light."[2]

At the same time, Howard's mother started showing signs of mental illness. His mother told him that he was "hideous," and that she wished to keep him locked in the house so people would not have to see him. This had a very negative effect on the young man, and he would continue to feel bad about the way she treated him well into his adulthood. He would later say that his mother's psychological abuse was devastating.[3]

Howard Lovecraft started to read the early pulp magazines of the day, especially *The Argosy*. Lovecraft sent a letter to *The Argosy* in 1913 attacking the stories of Fred Jackson. His letters started an in-print argument with other readers which lasted for several months. Lovecraft wrote most of his letters as poems, writing much like a man from the previous century. The debate came to the attention of Edward F. Daas, president of the United Amateur Press Association (UAPA), a group of amateur writers from around the country. Soon, Lovecraft joined the group and started publishing his own paper, *The Conservative*.

Lovecraft started writing fiction, including such horror stories as "The Tomb" and "Dagon," both in 1917. He built a network of friends with whom he wrote letters. Lovecraft soon had hundreds of friends, keeping in touch with them by mail. Lovecraft's letters were quirky and fun, and he would often sign them as "HPL" or "Grandpa Theobald." Though a young man, Lovecraft liked to think of himself as much older than he was.

One of the friends he made through letter writing was a very young writer named Robert Bloch. Lovecraft encouraged Bloch, and even put him in a story. In "The Haunter of the Dark" young "Robert Blake" uncovers a sinister cult in New England.

Lovecraft's mother had a nervous breakdown in 1919 and was admitted to Butler Hospital where, like her husband, she remained until she died. Sarah Susan Phillips died on May 24, 1921, during a gall bladder operation.

Soon after his mother's death, Lovecraft attended an amateur journalism convention in Boston. There he met Sonia Haft Green, who was seven years older than he. Lovecraft was living with his two aunts at the time, Lillian and Annie, but he would leave Providence to visit Sonia at her home in Brooklyn, New York. They were married on March 3, 1924; Lovecraft informed his aunts of his marriage by sending them a letter.

Lovecraft moved into Sonia's apartment in Brooklyn, and continued his work as a writer. Sonia had a successful hat shop on Fifth Avenue in New York City.

Most of Lovecraft's work appeared in the pulp magazine *Weird Tales*. It began publication in March

1923 and would continue until 1954. *Weird Tales* was an incredibly important publication for American horror fiction. Not only did *Weird Tales* publish the work of Lovecraft, but also the early stories of Robert Bloch, Ray Bradbury and Richard Matheson. Unlike today, there were few horror stories published as books; *Weird Tales* was just about the only market around for horror story writers.[4]

For his stories, Lovecraft invented a world all his own. Many tales formed his "Cthulhu Mythos" series: stories about a race of monsters beyond time and space. He also invented a lost book of dangerous magic, the accursed *Necronomicon*, "written" by Abdul Alhazred and held under lock and key in the library of the fictitious Miskatonic University.

Most of his stories took place in the fictional New England towns of Arkham and Dunwich, which later inspired Stephen King to create his own towns of 'Salem's Lot and Castle Rock. Readers were so convinced by Lovecraft's stories that they often wrote to him, asking about getting copies of the *Necronomicon*.

Lovecraft did not make a lot of money from writing for *Weird Tales,* and soon he and Sonia ran into financial trouble. Lovecraft tried to raise more money by "ghost writing" for others, including the famous magician Harry Houdini. Sonia's hat store went bankrupt and Lovecraft, who had never held a regular job, could not find work. On January 1, 1925, Sonia went to Cleveland when she was offered work there, and Lovecraft, who always preferred his own company, moved into a small apartment in Red Hook, Brooklyn.

Lovecraft missed Providence and hated Brooklyn. He became depressed and started to carry a bottle of poison with him. Worried over his mental state, his Aunt Lillian invited him to return to Providence in 1926.[5] Lovecraft's over-protective aunts barred Sonia from returning with him and, in 1929, they divorced.

The last few years of Lovecraft's life were full and happy ones. He wrote most of his greatest fiction,

For his stories, Lovecraft invented a world all his own.

including the stories "The Call of Cthulhu" (1926), "The Shadow Out of Time" (1935), and his novella *At the Mountains of Madness* (1931). He traveled to Quebec, Philadelphia, Charleston, and St. Augustine. He continued writing many letters.

In 1935 Lovecraft began to experience problems with his digestion. After suffering with digestive pain for two years, Lovecraft finally went to a doctor. He was diagnosed with colon cancer. He was admitted to the Jane Brown Memorial Hospital on March 10. The cancer had already advanced too far for surgery (he would have survived had he gone to a doctor two years earlier), and he died early on the morning of March 15. He was only forty-seven years old and was buried beside his parents.[6]

H. P. Lovecraft is among the most important American authors of horror stories. Though most of his stories were published in book form only after his death, they exerted a powerful hold on the public's imagination. Lovecraft's stories often dealt with a horror that was too large for ordinary people to understand—monsters bigger than time and space. Perhaps most important, Lovecraft's friendship and inspiration to younger authors helped a whole generation of horror readers become writers themselves.

Robert Bloch

Robert Bloch

(1917–1994)

Robert Bloch was a very funny man who wrote very suspenseful stories. For Bloch, the terrifying was often amusing, and he looked very much like a mischievous boy well into his old age. His sense of humor would often catch even the most careful listener off guard.

Bloch wrote more than two hundred short stories of horror, fantasy, science fiction, and crime. He also wrote twenty-two novels and many articles. Many people have seen his work in the movies or on television, as Bloch wrote for such television shows as *Star Trek* and *Alfred Hitchcock Presents*, and movies like *Torture Garden* and *The Night Walker*. Like Lovecraft, Bloch was an extremely generous man who answered all letters written to him by his readers, offering solid advice to young writers.

Bloch was born on April 5, 1917 in Chicago. His father, Raphael Bloch, was a bank cashier and his mother, Stella Loeb, was a social worker. As a child, Bloch often went to the movies. His happiest movie memories were of the mystery melodramas starring Lon Chaney. In the 1920s, movies were silent but had an organist playing live music in the theater. In 1925, Bloch saw Chaney in *The Phantom of the Opera.* Bloch was profoundly moved by the story of the disfigured musical genius who lived beneath the Paris Opera House. Bloch remembered that ". . . after the film had ended, the image that floated behind me was the Phantom's face. He kept me company in bed and haunted my dreams."[1]

Perhaps the most important influence on Bloch's boyhood was the discovery of *Weird Tales* magazine. In the summer of 1927, Bloch went with his family on a train trip to visit relatives. Bloch was given something to read on the trip and he became entranced by a magazine with stories with titles like "Satan's Fiddle," "Creeping Shadows," and "The Man with a Thousand Legs." Aunt Lil bought Bloch a copy of *Weird Tales* and it was a moment that would change his life.[2]

The Bloch family had a reversal of fortune when the Great Depression hit. The Depression was a period of high unemployment and widespread poverty. Robert's father, Raphael Bloch lost his job and the family moved to Milwaukee, where they lived in a cramped, three-room apartment. In Milwaukee, Stella Bloch found work at a local settlement house, and Raphael Bloch eventually found work as a cashier in a cafeteria.

While in high school Bloch still read *Weird Tales*. The local magazine store only bought two copies of the magazine, and Bloch would get up the first day of each month at 6:30 in the morning to rush down to the store and buy one. Bloch greatly enjoyed the stories of H. P. Lovecraft, and he started corresponding with the older writer in 1933.

Lovecraft encouraged young Bloch to write stories of his own, and also offered to read some of them and provide advice. After Bloch wrote several stories in Lovecraft's style, Lovecraft suggested that he send one, "Lilies," to a magazine called *Marvel Tales*. Bloch did and, at seventeen, became a published author. A few months later, Bloch sold his story "The Secret of the Tomb" to *Weird Tales*.

Writing for *Weird Tales* only paid one penny a word, but Bloch planned to write many more stories for the magazine. As he remembered in his memoirs, "if I could step up my output, perhaps in five or six years I'd make enough money to starve to death."[3]

In 1935, Bloch wrote "The Shambler from the Stars," which featured a character much like Lovecraft who was killed at the end. Lovecraft was so amused by the idea that he killed off Bloch (called "Blake"). Blake is a character Lovecraft created in the story,

"The Haunter of the Dark." Lovecraft dedicated the story to the young writer, the only time Lovecraft ever did that.

Determined to continue as a professional writer, Bloch published short stories in the pulps, and also wrote for vaudeville shows and for political candidates.

On October 2, 1940, Bloch married Marion Ruth Holcomb. Bloch continued to make a meager income with his writing, selling stories to such magazines as *Unknown Worlds and Fantastic Adventures*. Bloch also worked as a copywriter for the Gustav Marx ad agency to help make ends meet. In 1943, Bloch and Marion had their only child, a daughter named Sally.

In those days before television, radio presented a great deal of America's popular entertainment. Many radio shows had recurring characters like the Shadow or Superman week-after-week, but "anthology" programs had different stories with different characters every week.

Horror shows were among the most popular anthology programs on radio. Shows like *Light's Out*, *Inner Sanctum*, and *The Witch's Tale* told stories calculated to raise goosebumps. Bloch and some of his friends thought they could do just as well, and created a program called *Stay Tuned For Terror*.

Bloch adapted many of his early stories for this program, and arranged with *Weird Tales* to publicize the show in the pages of the magazine. In his autobiography, Bloch remembered the experience as a very pleasant one.

In 1945, Bloch published his first two collections of short stories, *Sea-Kissed* and *The Opener of the Way.* The second book was published by Arkham House, a publishing house named after a fictional town mentioned in the stories of H. P. Lovecraft.

Bloch soon turned his attention toward writing a novel. He wrote *The Scarf* in 1947, about a psychopathic writer who is also a serial killer. This was, in many ways, a dramatic change from the way horror fiction was written. Previously, horror stories relied on a supernatural menace. With *The Scarf,* Bloch became a specialist in stories of real-life terror: the quiet neighbor who is secretly a mad killer.[4]

Since their marriage, Marion had suffered from a leg problem that seriously affected her health. In 1953, Bloch left the Marx agency and moved his family to Weyauwega, Wisconsin. While there, he would write many short stories and four novels: *Spiderweb, The Kidnapper, The Will to Kill,* and *Shooting Star.*

In 1959, Bloch wrote the novel that changed his life forever. It was called *Psycho.* In the story, a quiet young man named Norman Bates runs an isolated hotel off the main highway. Guests who check-in to the Bates Motel have a way of never coming out again, and the only person who may know the true story is Norman's mother.

Psycho received several good reviews, and Bloch's agent received a bid for the film rights from a Hollywood production company. The rights were sold for $9,500. It was only after he received the money that Bloch learned that the famous director, Alfred Hitchcock, operated the production company.

The screenplay for *Psycho* was extremely close to Bloch's novel. Although most new movies at that time were made with color film, Hitchcock produced the film in black-and-white to create a sinister mood, and the finished product is considered to be one of the classics of the horror film.[5]

After the success of *Psycho*, Bloch went to Hollywood to write scripts for movies and television shows. He wrote the scripts for two films, *The Couch* and *The Cabinet of Caligari*, the remake of a German silent film. In Hollywood, Bloch also wrote for the television horror show *Thriller*, which was hosted by Boris Karloff. (Karloff was the actor who played the Frankenstein monster in a series of three films made during the 1930s). Bloch wrote ten episodes of *Thriller* during its 1960–1962 run, and considered it to be his best work for television.

In October, 1963, Robert and Marion divorced. She was unhappy with life in California and the pressures of his heavy workload. Soon after the divorce, Bloch would meet and marry Eleanor Alexander. They remained married for the rest of his life.

For the next several years, Bloch continued to work in television and movies. Some of his screenplays included *Strait-Jacket* (1964), *The Skull* (1965), *The Psychopath* (1968) and *Torture Garden* (1968). He also wrote several science-fiction novels, including

Robert Bloch (right) is shown with author Bob Madison at the Famous Monsters Convention in Washington, D. C., in May 1993.

Ladies Day and *This Crowded Earth, Sneak Preview,* and *It's All in Your Mind.* In addition, Bloch found time to write a television film about a madman who created an army of zombies, *The Dead Don't Die* (1975).

In 1978, Bloch wrote a novel to honor his old friend, H. P. Lovecraft. The book, *Strange Eons,* tells of a group of people who discover that Lovecraft's stories were "real," and find the world threatened by a race of monsters.

Bloch wrote a sequel to *Psycho* in 1982, called *Psycho II.* In it, Norman Bates escapes from the asylum just before filmmakers start a movie based on his life. Bloch would do another follow-up, called *Psycho House* (1990), where the Bates Motel becomes a tourist attraction.

In his latter years, Bloch wrote his autobiography, *Once Around the Bloch.* His sense of humor was as strong as ever, for he subtitled the book, *An Unauthorized Autobiography.*

Robert Bloch died on September 23, 1994, of cancer. Bloch took horror out of the gothic castles of Poe and antique towns of Lovecraft and brought it up-to-date. Though there are many vampires, werewolves and ghouls in Bloch's stories, his monsters are often people right next door, like Norman Bates. Bloch saw the horror in the everyday and helped place horror stories in a recognizable, modern American setting. His stories will always be popular with people who like a good scare.

Shirley Jackson
(1919–1965)

Shirley Jackson was born on December 14, 1919. Her parents, Leslie and Geraldine Jackson, were a wealthy couple living in San Francisco. When Shirley was two, the family moved thirty miles away to Burlingame, California.

Jackson became a writer as soon as she could write. Young Jackson wrote poems, and would amuse her mother with her ability to make up rhymes. She was also an active girl, and Jackson divided her time between reading, writing and sports. By the time Jackson had entered Burlingame High School in 1931, she had written many poems and short stories.[1]

Shirley wrote through all of high school, and enrolled in the liberal arts program at the University of Rochester in New York in 1934. However, Jackson

Shirley Jackson (center) is shown with her husband, Stanley Edgar Hyman (right) and Professor Donald Dike at the Festival of Arts at Syracuse University, Syracuse, New York, in 1965.

soon grew depressed at college. She suffered long bouts of unhappiness, and questioned the loyalty of her friends. Jackson left the university before graduating.[2]

Jackson spent the next year writing and doing very little else. She established a schedule for her writing work, and she would follow it for the rest of her life. By the time this year of intensive writing was over, Jackson had taught herself the discipline necessary to be a writer.

Jackson thought it would be a good idea to continue her education, and she entered Syracuse University in New York in 1937. She wanted to study writing and started in the university's School of Journalism. Soon, however, she transferred to the English department. During the next two years at Syracuse, Jackson published fifteen stories and articles in school magazines. She also became editor of *The Syracusan*, a campus humor magazine.

Later, Jackson and her fellow classmate Stanley Edgar Hyman, created their own literary magazine, *The Spectre*. The first issue came out in 1939. Although the magazine was very popular with students, teachers in the English department did not like many of Jackson's editorials which were critical of them and the school.[3]

While in school, Jackson also met Professor Leonard Brown, who taught modern literature. He approved of Jackson's efforts with *The Spectre*, and he backed the students and the publication. Jackson would always think of Brown as a mentor and inspiration, and later dedicated her book *The Haunting of Hill House* to him.

When Jackson and Hyman graduated in 1940, the school stopped publication of *The Spectre*. School authorities were still upset over some of the views expressed in the magazine. The school's anger toward her lasted throughout her career: the school did not award her with the Arents Pioneer Medal (the honor granted to successful former students) until 1965. At that time, Jackson was too sick to attend the ceremony.

Once out of school, Jackson and Hyman married. They lived in Vermont, and the small towns of New England would serve as the setting for some of Jackson's most famous work. She worked steadily, writing her first novel, *The Road Through the Wall*, between 1945 and 1947.

Shirley Jackson became famous in 1948 with the publication of her short story, "The Lottery." It first appeared in the magazine, *The New Yorker*. "The Lottery" remains one of the most controversial pieces of fiction the magazine ever published. "The Lottery" takes place in a small American town much like many others. The residents gather once a year for a lottery—but with horrifying results for the winner.

The story was later turned into a one-act play, and the tale is still read often on the radio and at literary events. It was adapted for television in 1952, and is found in many school libraries and anthologies. *The New Yorker* received hundreds of letters when the story appeared, letters which Jackson said contained "bewilderment, speculation and plain old-fashioned abuse."[4]

Jackson managed to work while raising four children: Laurence, Sarah, Joanne and Barry. Jackson sold stories to most of the popular magazines of the day, including *Collier's* and *Reader's Digest.* In 1949, the family moved to Westport, Connecticut and the following year, Jackson published her second novel, *Hangsaman*, to very good reviews. The book is about a confused college girl who creates an imaginary female friend. In the end, the heroine must choose between reality and fantasy.

Hangsaman marked the beginning of a period during which Jackson did most of her writing. During the 1950s she published forty-four short stories, six articles, two books about her family, four novels and a children's book. Jackson greatly enjoyed writing a nonfiction book, *The Witchcraft of Salem Village*, in 1956. This book, for readers aged twelve to fourteen, came about after Jackson joked that she had witchlike traits. It is a simple account of the witch trials of 1692–1693. In 1958, Jackson wrote *The Sundial*, a novel about a group of people who wait in a gothic castle for the end of the world to come.

It was also during these years that Jackson started to suffer from the anxiety that would become a problem as she grew older.[5] She disliked leaving her home, and often felt ill at ease. When Jackson was not involved in one of her many lecture tours, she liked to stay at home, where she felt happy and safe.

In 1959 Jackson wrote *The Haunting of Hill House*. It was a significant literary success, and received excellent reviews. It would be adapted into a major motion picture in 1963, *The Haunting*, and remade, not as successfully, in 1999.

The story traces the events that follow when a group of psychic researchers stay in a deserted home, Hill House. Throughout its ninety-year history, Hill House has been the scene of unhappiness and tragedy. One of the women in the group, Eleanor, finds herself strangely at home in Hill House. Jackson never shows the reader her ghosts, and all the manifestations of the supernatural may be in Eleanor's mind.

Jackson got the idea for her story after reading a book about a group of nineteenth century psychic researchers who rented a haunted house to study it. Jackson searched through a variety of newspapers, magazines, and books for pictures of old, abandoned houses that looked haunted. When she found a picture of a California home that had just the right spooky look, she

Shirley Jackson is seen here in her college yearbook photograph.

sent it to her mother to do some research on it. To Jackson's surprise, her mother wrote back to say that her great-grandfather had built it![6]

Through the years, Jackson gained a great deal of weight. She suffered from asthma and arthritis. Also, her bouts of anxiety steadily got worse. Jackson went regularly to a psychiatrist for help, but still sank into a depression. She managed to keep working and wrote stories as another form of therapy.[7]

In 1959, Jackson started work on her book *We Have Always Lived in the Castle.* When it was published in 1962, *Time* magazine called it the best novel of the year. In that book two sisters, Constance and Merricat, are victimized by their small New England town following the unsolved murder of their family.

After years of therapy, Jackson's anxiety started to lessen. She saw the psychiatrist less and less frequently. However, as her mind improved her body continued to decline. On the afternoon of August 8, 1965, Jackson, only forty-six years old, went upstairs to take a nap. She died in her sleep of a heart attack.

Jackson was one of the very first writers of horror stories to be taken seriously by literary critics while still alive, and one of the few women to write tales of terror. Jackson's treatment of mental illness in her stories echo challenges she faced in real life and her fiction will be remembered for its elegant prose and depiction of complex characters.

Rod Serling

Rod Serling

(1924–1975)

His face and voice are among the most famous in television history. Once a week for five years, Rod Serling appeared on television reading this elegant introduction:

> There is a fifth dimension beyond that which is known to man. It is a dimension as vast as space and as timeless as infinity. It is the middle ground between the pit of man's fears and the summit of his knowledge. It is the dimension of the imagination. It is an area we call . . . The Twilight Zone.[1]

The success of the television series, *The Twilight Zone,* made Serling as well known and widely recognized for his face and his voice, as he was for his writing.

Rodman Edward Serling was born in Syracuse, New York, on December 25, 1924. His father, Samuel Lawrence Serling, owned a wholesale meat business and his mother, Esther, was a housewife. Soon after Rod was born, the family moved to Binghamton, New York, where Rod would spend the rest of his boyhood.

Rod was an outgoing boy. He made friends easily, and he loved to talk. Often he talked so much, his family would sometimes be annoyed by it. Once, while the family was taking a two and a half hour car trip from Binghamton to Syracuse, the Serling family promised each other to stay quiet until six year old Rod stopped talking. Rod never did grow quiet, he talked and chatted and questioned and sang for the entire trip without anyone else saying anything![2]

After Rod graduated high school in 1943, he was drafted into the Army 11th Airborne Division Paratroopers. He made extra money as a boxer; only five-foot four, Serling was classed as a flyweight. He would box eighteen fights and lose only one. Serling was sent to the Philippine Islands during World War II, and was wounded during battle. Loose pieces of metal called shrapnel hit him in the leg and the wrist. While he was recovering from his injuries, his father died of a heart attack in 1945.

Discharged from the army, Serling returned to the United States in 1946 and enrolled in Antioch College in Yellow Springs, Ohio. He originally intended to study physical education but soon switched his college major to language and literature.

Serling found that writing was an important outlet for him after the stresses and depression he faced during and after the war. Serling believed writing was a "therapeutic necessity," and that writing about his feelings made him realize that his future was as a professional writer.[3] Serling wrote for the school radio station and soon his script *To Live a Dream* won second prize in a national script writing contest. Serling won $500 and an all expense paid trip to New York. It was also in 1946 that Serling met Carolyn Louise Kramer, who was also a student at Antioch College. They soon fell in love, and were married in July, 1948.

After college, Serling earned a living by testing experimental parachutes for the army. In the spring of 1948, Serling was offered $1,000 to test one of the Army Air Forces' new jet ejection seats. Serling's friend, Don Scobel, became worried when the young writer did not make his return train after the test. He waited until late that night when a train arrived, carrying Serling, covered in enough bandages to wrap a mummy. Serling would later tell friends that three other volunteers were killed in similar tests before he succeeded.[4]

The Serlings moved to Cincinnati where Rod became a staff writer for WLW radio. Serling was not very happy there because radio executives told him that they wanted characters who could "get their teeth into the soil." Serling would later say, "What those guys wanted wasn't a writer, but a plow."[5] Serling continued his freelance fiction writing and collected forty rejection slips in a row from magazines. He knew he wanted to be a creative writer, but the steady money of writing for radio held him back.

Serling's luck changed in 1949 when he sold two radio scripts and his first television script, "Grady Everett for the People," to a program called *Stars Over Hollywood*. He received $100 for it.

In the early 1950s, many television programs were anthology shows. These shows had no recurring characters, and told different stories every week. In 1951, Serling was able to sell enough scripts to anthology programs to earn $5,000—a lot of money for that time. Serling left the radio station and started writing television plays full time. By 1955, Serling had sold more than seventy television scripts. In January of that year, Serling's teleplay "Patterns" was broadcast. The show was about the in-fighting inside a large American corporation. "Patterns" won Serling an Emmy Award for best writer.

Serling continued writing for television, scoring another hit with *Requiem for a Heavyweight* in 1956. This story of a broken-down boxer who eventually fights in "fixed" matches won Serling another Emmy, the Television-Radio Writer's Annual Award for Writing Achievement, the Sylvania Award, and the George Foster Peabody Award. Serling won another Emmy in 1957 for his teleplay, *The Comedians*.

Still, Serling wanted more freedom to write what he wanted. He felt that television sponsors changed his ideas too often, toning down some of Serling's thoughts and feelings on contemporary issues. Serling realized that he could write about issues that were important to him if he disguised his ideas as fantasy stories. To do this, Serling created *The Twilight Zone.*[6]

The Twilight Zone debuted on October 2, 1959, on CBS. The ratings were extremely low, but studio executives thought the show had enough quality to keep it on the air. It would last one hundred and fifty-six episodes, ending its run in the summer of 1965.

On one level, *The Twilight Zone* told simple stories of horror and fantasy. But on a deeper level, Serling used the show as a means of writing about things that concerned him. At different times, *The Twilight Zone* explored such themes as racism, nuclear war, mass hysteria, and, what is beautiful and what is ugly. Because the show was an anthology, Serling was able to tell many different types of stories, including ghost stories, spooky westerns, tales of the future and examinations of life on other planets. Serling wrote ninety-two of the scripts, the remaining sixty-four scripts were written by such respected horror and science-fiction writers as Ray Bradbury, Richard Matheson and Charles Beaumont.

The Twilight Zone is part of television history, and the name itself is a catchphrase. Creating *The Twilight*

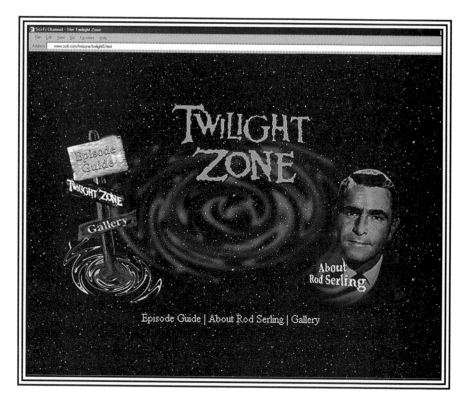

The Twilight Zone debuted on October 2, 1959 on CBS. It would last one hundred and fifty-six episodes, ending its run in the summer of 1965.

Zone was not always easy. CBS often threatened to cancel *The Twilight Zone* due to low ratings, and once changed its running time from thirty minutes to one hour. Despite it all, Serling was able to win another two Emmy Awards for his writing on the show. The show was finally canceled in 1965 due to poor ratings.

The pace of writing, producing and narrating a weekly television program was grueling, even for a workaholic like Serling. He soon had to start dictating his scripts to his secretary, and he would smoke as many as four packs of cigarettes while working.[7]

To his surprise, Serling found himself to be something of a star. He found steady work narrating such programs as *The Undersea World of Jacques Cousteau,* providing voice-overs for television specials, and starring in television commercials. Despite his success, Serling yearned to go back to serious television writing.

In 1968, Serling became the host of a television horror show called *The Night Gallery.* He did not have complete control over the program, as he did for *The Twilight Zone.* Serling was unhappy with the quality of the show. *The Night Gallery* lasted until 1972, but it never attained the success of *The Twilight Zone.*

The grind of writing for television had taken its toll on Serling. He began to age physically, and his face became prematurely wrinkled. On his fortieth birthday, Serling made his first parachute jump since World War II to prove that he was not old.[8] Serling would make comments about feeling older than his age for the last ten years of his life. Unfortunately, Serling never realized the impact of *The Twilight Zone*. "When I look back over thirty years of professional writing, I'm hard-pressed to come up with anything that's important," he said. "Some things are literate, some things are interesting, some things are classy, but very damn little is important."[9]

In May 1975, Serling suffered a mild heart attack while on summer vacation at Interlake, New York. He stayed in the hospital for two weeks, and was told to quit smoking, work less, and exercise. The following month, Serling was admitted to Strong Memorial Hospital in Rochester for heart bypass surgery. He had another heart attack during surgery and died. He was only fifty years old.

Rod Serling was the first writer of horror stories to become a multimedia star. Not only was he famous for writing, but he was famous for his appearances on *The Twilight Zone*, on game shows and commercials, and for his work narrating television specials and documentaries. Serling's humanism is evident in all of his stories, which have socially or morally relevant themes. Serling was wrong about his work being forgotten: *The Twilight Zone* is still seen in reruns around the world.

Dean Koontz
(1945–)

Among the earliest memories Dean Koontz has are of sleepless hours spent in his dark, cramped bedroom, planning elaborate escapes or fantasizing about a life at sea with pirates. His retreat into fantasy was necessary, as it was one way to avoid his unstable and alcoholic father.[1]

Dean Ray Koontz was born on July 9, 1945, in Everett, Pennsylvania. He was the only child of Ray and Florence Koontz. When Dean was a boy, the family moved to Bedford, also in Pennsylvania. In Bedford, Dean had a very unhappy childhood—his father often drank and became violent. Even as an adult, Dean Koontz is completely unable to recall one happy memory of his father.

Dean Koontz

Fortunately, not all of Koontz's memories are bad. Among his happiest childhood memories are reading *The Martian Chronicles*, by Ray Bradbury. He also discovered books by Robert Heinlein and H.G. Wells, and watched old horror movies with actors like Bela Lugosi and Boris Karloff. Koontz believes that the desire to become a writer sprang from the need to provide people with the same emotional release that he got from books during this difficult time of his life.[2]

The Koontz family was very poor. Dean's father and uncle would hunt deer, rabbits and squirrels to provide food for the family. The water was heated by a kerosene burner in the basement. One of Koontz's chores was to get five gallon cans of kerosene and relight the burner. He was always sure it would set on fire. Unlike most American homes, the Koontz house did not even have indoor plumbing. The family bathroom was an outhouse at the end of the backyard.

In spite of his childhood difficulties, Koontz remained bright and optimistic. Koontz does not believe that people must stay prisoners to the bad things that happened in their lives. He feels that there are always possibilities for success and happiness. Aside from being scary and suspenseful, Koontz's books are also often funny. "If some of my books, in some small way, help people to find the will and strength to get past the effects of disastrous childhoods, that alone makes writing worthwhile."[3]

Koontz started to make his own books when he was eight or nine years old. He wrote and illustrated his own stories, and then stapled them together, hiding the staples with tape. Koontz then sold his stories to family members.

Koontz did not do well in school. He passed the courses that interested him and just managed to get by on those that did not. He read a great deal, and became an expert on those things that touched his imagination, such as comics and horror stories. When he was a senior in high school, Koontz met his future wife, Gerda. They married three and a half years later, when he finished college. All they had was $300, a used car, and some clothes.

While Koontz was still in college, he won a fiction contest sponsored by the *Atlantic Monthly* with a short story about a little girl who drowns her new baby siblings. After college, Koontz worked as a counselor in the Appalachian Poverty Program for a year, writing at night. The Poverty Program was designed to distribute federal money to one of the poorest areas of the United States. Koontz grew frustrated with the program and left after one year.

After leaving the Poverty Program, Koontz taught English for a year and a half in Mechanicsburg, Pennsylvania. During this time, Koontz sold three poorly distributed paperback science-fiction novels that did not help build his reputation and about twenty short stories.

Gerda saw that Koontz was worried about his chances of becoming a writer and offered to support him for five years while he tried to build a writing career. "If you can't make it in five years," she said, "you never will."[4] Koontz quit his job and worked sixty hour weeks, writing science-fiction novels and horror stories. Five years later, Gerda quit her job and managed the business side of Koontz's career.

During this time, Koontz wrote novels like *Star Quest* (1968) and *Time Thieves* (1972), which were action-filled science-fiction stories. His last science-fiction novel was *Demon Seed* (1973). It was made into a successful movie in 1977. The more Koontz wrote, the more his craft as a writer developed.

In 1969, Koontz's mother died from multiple strokes. She was only fifty-three at the time. His father lived an additional twenty-two years. For the last fourteen years of his father's life, Koontz was the sole support of his father. Ray Koontz was diagnosed with a mental disorder, schizophrenia, complicated by alcoholism. Twice, Koontz was almost stabbed to death by his father, and had to struggle to disarm him. Ray Koontz would die at age eighty-one.[5]

After only a few years, Koontz grew tired of writing science-fiction and wanted to move on. He had written many different types of books, including suspense stories, romances and horror novels, including *The Funhouse* (1980), *The Mask* (1981), and *Darkfall* (1984).

It was during the 1980s that Koontz created some of his most popular and important books.[6] *Phantoms* (1980) is one of Koontz's most horrific novels, and also contains touches of science-fiction. *The Eyes of Darkness* (1981) concerns the death of a child that might have been faked to cover a kidnapping. *The House of Thunder* (1982) is about Susan, who has lost her memory, and is surrounded by sinister characters who are not what they pretend to be. *Twilight Eyes* (1985) deals with Slim MacKenzie, who has "twilight eyes," the ability to see the goblins that live among us, disguised as humans.

In 1991 Dean and Gerda Koontz moved to Newport Beach, California, where they live today. They have a comfortable home with a view of the Pacific Ocean. There, Koontz wakes up at seven-thirty, exercises, and then works from ten o'clock in the morning until seven-thirty or eight o'clock at night. He usually has lunch at his desk, eating as he works.

The wild imagination of Dean Koontz has continued into the 1990s. One of Koontz's most successful books of this decade was *Dragon Tears* (1993). In it a psychotic killer—the Ticktock man—plans to murder two agents from a special police team. Ticktock's threat is a serious one: he can make unstoppable monsters from common dirt and can manipulate time and space. Other books written in the 1990s include *The Bad Place* (1990), *Mr. Murder* (1993), and *Winter Moon* (1994). *The Bad Place* includes a

Aside from being scary and suspenseful, Koontz's books are often funny.

character named Thomas, who is disabled with Down's Syndrome. Many scenes in the book are from Thomas' point of view. Other books include *Dark Rivers of the Heart* (1994), *Strange Highways* (1995), and *Intensity* (1997). In 1999, Koontz released *Seize the Night*, a story about a missing child and a secret laboratory base where scientists are working on germ warfare.

In the future, Koontz hopes to maintain his good health, and yearns to develop more as a writer, moving along to even more interesting books. That, he says, would be "paradise."[7]

For years, Dean Koontz had his feet planted in two important literary traditions: science fiction and horror. After he stopped writing science fiction with his novel *Demon Seed,* Koontz has produced a series of horror stories that are more than just tales calculated to frighten. Instead, Koontz writes books that blend suspense, romance, reality, and horror.

R. L. Stine
(1943–   )

When he was growing up, Bob Stine shared a bedroom with his younger brother, Bill. Overhead was the attic, which their parents had declared off limits. The boys would often lay awake at night, making up stories about the things hidden up there. The stories were often scary, and Bob would leave his brother in suspense before finishing the tale.

When Bob was seven and his family planned to move, he finally crept up into the attic. There was nothing there except for a clothes rack and a small black case. He took the case downstairs and discovered it held a typewriter. Stine quickly learned to type using one finger, a method he still uses to this

R. L. Stine

day. He also started writing stories. In time, he became one of the world's best-selling authors.[1]

Robert Lawrence Stine was born on October 8, 1943, in Columbus, Ohio. He does not remember his childhood being particularly scary, but he did have a wonderful talent for creating horror stories. He would regale his brother and friends with horror stories. Favorite stories would involve vampires, werewolves and ghosts.

Bob Stine was raised in Bexley, a suburb of Columbus. Bob was obsessed with comic books, and he would write and illustrate his own. He also read *MAD*, a humor magazine, and he realized that he liked laughing almost as much as he liked being scared. He created his own humor magazines, *The All New Bob Stine Giggle Book* and *HAH, For Maniacs Only!!* on his portable typewriter. These magazines contained parodies of famous television shows of the time and Bob would pass them around to his friends at school. Of all the magazines Bob created, his favorite was *BARF*, which was made up of funny captions under photographs he had cut from magazines. Bob's friends thought these magazines were wonderfully funny, but his teachers often thought otherwise.[2]

Bob also liked to go to see horror movies, especially the science-fiction films with bug-eyed monsters. He also loved television's *The Twilight Zone*, written and narrated by Rod Serling, and books by authors such as Isaac Asimov and Ray Bradbury.[3] When interviewed, Stine later said that

Bradbury's 1962 novel *Something Wicked This Way Comes* is the scariest book he has ever read.[4] Another favorite were EC comic-books.

EC had such titles as *Tales from the Crypt, The Vault of Horror* and *Weird Science.* These comics were often gruesome, but sometimes also darkly funny. Many parents and teachers, however, thought that these comics were a bad influence on children. Finally, after a few years, the comic industry created the Comics Code Authority. The Code toned-down the scary aspects of the stories. In time, the popularity of horror comics declined and most of the great horror comics eventually stopped publication.[5]

Bob's mother thought *MAD* magazine and the horror comics were trash. She would not let him bring them into the house. When he noticed that the books were always around the barbershop, Bob went to get a haircut every week.

Bob was popular in high school and he made comedy tapes featuring funny voices and gags with friends on his tape recorder. It was also when he was in high school that Stine started writing his first novel, an adult animal comedy called *Lovable Bear.* That book was never published, but Bob started to learn how to construct an interesting story. He regularly entered essay contests and took every opportunity he could to learn to be a better writer.

Stine attended Ohio State University in 1959 while living at home. He wrote for the campus magazine, *Sundial.* Stine used many of the tricks he had learned making comedy magazines as a boy and wrote joke articles for publication. He often ran pictures of scary characters from films like *House on Haunted Hill* and said the person in the picture was a campus official. Stine hoped that his jokes would draw attention to unfair school rules.[6]

Stine also unofficially ran for school president when he was a senior—knowing he would not be there to serve next year. His slogan was *Elect a Clown for President—Jovial Bob.* Stine notes with amusement in his autobiography that even though he was not on the ballot, he received 1,163 votes out of 8,727!

Stine graduated from Ohio State in 1965 and spent a year teaching history at a nearby high school. He allowed kids who behaved from Monday through Thursday to read all day Friday. Often, Stine would join his students on Friday, reading comic-books. Teaching gave Stine a chance to watch kids up close, and he incorporated much of what he learned into his two popular series, *Goosebumps* and *Fear Street.*

Stine then moved to New York to fulfill his life-long ambition to become a full-time writer. He moved into a tiny apartment in Greenwich Village and lived on bologna sandwiches. His first job was working in the art department of an investment magazine, but he was soon fired. His next job was writing. He invented celebrity interviews for $100 a week.

Stine was hired as an editor at Scholastic Books in 1968, and became editor and chief writer of *Bananas,*

When he was young, R. L. Stine loved television's *The Twilight Zone,* written and narrated by Rod Serling, and books by authors such as Isaac Asimov and Ray Bradbury.

Scholastic's humor magazine. Stine worked at Scholastic for sixteen years. In addition to writing most of the articles, he also wrote his first children's book, *How to Be Funny*. To publicize the book, he appeared at a New York bookstore to sign autographs wearing a pair of rabbit ears. That afternoon he sold and autographed only one book.

Stine met Jane Waldhorn at a party in Brooklyn. They quickly fell in love, and two weeks later they decided to get married. They were married on June 22, 1969. The couple had a son, Matthew Daniel Stine, on June 7, 1980. During the first decade of his marriage, Stine wrote books about Indiana Jones, James Bond and G.I. Joe. He also worked as chief writer for *Eureeka's Castle*, a program seen on Nickelodeon.

In 1984, Stine was having lunch with Jean Feiwel, Scholastic's editorial director. She suggested that he write a horror novel especially for young people. That book, *Blind Date*, was published by Scholastic in 1986 and became a best seller. *Blind Date* is a story about a boy who gets mysterious phone calls from a dead girl who wants to be his blind date.

A year later, Scholastic asked him to write another horror novel. Stine called it *Twisted*, and it is about a sorority house filled with girls who had to commit murder once a year. He followed that with *The Babysitter*; all three books became best sellers.

Stine decided to create a whole series of horror books and came up with the name *Fear Street* while staring out of the window. The series officially started in 1989 with *The New Girl*, and it was a runaway success.

While working on *Fear Street*, Stine thought even younger kids would enjoy horror stories, too. Reading *TV Guide* one morning, he came across an ad for a horror movie marathon: "It's GOOSE-BUMPS Week on Channel 11!" He decided to call his new series *Goosebumps*. He wrote the first book in the series, *Welcome to Dead House*, in about ten days. Because of the immense popularity of the *Fear Street* and *Goosebumps* series, Stine has become one of the best selling authors in the world.

In 1995, Stine wrote his first horror novel for adults, *Superstitious*. He received a $1 million advance, some of which he gave to a program that sends inner-city students to prep schools. Today, Stine and his family live in New York City. He still writes the *Fear Street* and *Goosebumps* series, and plans on writing horror stories until his fans stop reading them.

Young people have always liked horror stories. With *Goosebumps*, R. L. Stine created horror stories expressly for young people, building a whole new audience for things that go bump in the night. Stine also created a merchandising giant, with *Goosebumps* knapsacks, tote bags, binders, and toys to delight children of all ages.

Anne Rice

(1941–   )

Anne Rice named herself.

Anne Rice was born Howard Allen O'Brien on October 4, 1941 at Marcy Hospital in New Orleans, Louisiana. She was the second of four daughters of Katherine and Howard O'Brien. When he was a child, Anne's father was called "Howard the coward" by school bullies who thought the name was girlish. It was on her first day at Redemptorist School, a Catholic school in New Orleans, when a nun asked little Howard what her name was. In a split second she blurted out "It's Anne!" Her mother later said, "if she wants to be Anne, then it's Anne."[1]

Katherine O'Brien, Anne's mother, made a point of never stifling her children's creativity, and encouraged

Anne Rice

them to be artistic. Sometimes, that even meant she let them draw on the walls. However, Katherine was also a very troubled person who was an alcoholic. To this day, Rice still remembers the pain of growing up with an alcoholic parent.

Anne and her family lived on the edge of the Garden District of New Orleans. Her father worked for the post office and wrote stories in his spare time. While growing up, Rice would wander around the Garden District, imagining how people lived in the big houses. In the seventh grade she wrote her first "book," filling up a whole notebook with a story about aliens who come to earth and eventually commit suicide.

When Anne was fifteen years old, her mother died of alcohol-related illnesses. At first Anne was relieved that her mother was no longer suffering. Then, Anne felt that something had been ripped out of her. "She gave me the belief in myself that I could do great things, that I could do anything I wanted to do."[2] Anne's father eventually remarried and moved the whole family to Richardson, Texas. Anne was very much against moving, but, because she was only sixteen, she had no choice.

Anne went to Richardson High and soon met Stan Rice in a journalism class. Stan was a year younger and a junior; he had also recently moved to Richardson from Dallas, Texas. Stan was used to sitting in the front of the class, but moved further back to sit beside Anne. Stan became editor of the school paper and Anne wrote articles for it. They were very good friends in school, but did not begin to date until after Anne graduated.

Anne went to Texas Women's College in Denton in 1959. In 1960 Stan followed her to Denton, but Anne wanted to live in San Francisco, California. The two decided that, for the time being, they would live in different cities and write to one another. Missing her, Stan sent Anne a telegram, proposing marriage. Anne returned to Texas and the two of them married on October 14, 1961.

Anne Rice returned to San Francisco with her husband and settled in a section of town called Haight-Ashbury. This was a time when many young Americans became involved in different cultures, living like "beatnicks" or "hippies," but Rice was too much of an individualist to be a part of it.[3] Rice took courses at the University of San Francisco, where she earned a degree in political science. At this time, 1965, Rice published her first short story, "October 4, 1948." The story concerns a girl who steps into an old, deserted house of the type Rice knew in New Orleans. Realizing that there are no ghosts, the girl leaves, no longer afraid.

On September 21, 1966, Anne gave birth to her first child, a baby girl named Michele. Stan also started teaching at San Francisco State University and Anne Rice started graduate school that year. She continued to grow as a writer, publishing the first chapter of her novel, *Nicholas and Jean*, in *Transfer* magazine. Encouraged by this success, Rice wrote more, concentrating on stories set in old New Orleans.

In 1969 the Rice family moved to Berkeley, California. Rice wrote a short story called "Interview with the Vampire," but could not interest any magazine publishers.

In 1970, Michele was diagnosed with leukemia, a form of cancer. Rice cared for her daughter and managed to get her master's degree in creative writing. Michele grew steadily worse and the family sank into despair. Two years later, Stan received a grant from the National Endowment for the Arts. The Rice family used the money to take Michele to Disneyland. Sadly, Michele Rice died on August 5, 1972, just before her sixth birthday.

Anne and Stan began to drink heavily, and she was afraid that she might become an alcoholic like her mother. Stan suggested that Anne become a full-time writer as a way of helping herself heal. She wrote at night in a corner of the bedroom while her husband slept. When she was finished, what she had written was the novel-length version of *Interview with the Vampire*.

Even though *Interview* would become an international bestseller, it was not easy for Rice to get it published. At first, publishers rejected it. Rice then went to a conference in 1974 and met an agent there who sold the book to Knopf in 1976.

Interview with the Vampire is considered to be the most popular vampire story of the twentieth century.[4] The main character is Louis, who narrates his life story to a journalist in contemporary San Francisco. Louis became a vampire in New Orleans in 1791 after being bitten by a vampire named Lestat. The two would raise a vampire child, named Claudia. This child is one of the most interesting characters in vampire literature. Writing about Claudia helped Rice come to grips with the intense grief she felt at the loss of her child.[5]

The Rices used some of the money earned by *Interview* to go on a world trip, visiting Europe, Egypt, Port-au-Prince, and other places. In 1977, Rice learned she was going to have another child. On March 11, 1978, she gave birth to a son, Christopher. Rice stopped drinking during her pregnancy and, on Memorial Day, 1979, Stan and Anne promised to never drink again.

In 1985, Rice continued the adventures of her fictional vampires with *The Vampire Lestat*. It was an incredible success. She followed it with another sequel, *Queen of the Damned* (1988), in which she told her own version of the complete history of vampirism. The vampire Lestat returned in *The Tale of the Body Thief* (1992).

In 1989 she left vampires and witches behind to write *The Mummy, or Ramses the Damned*, which she originally intended for a screenplay. That year, the Rice family moved back to her beloved New Orleans

Anne Rice wrote many books, including *The Vampire Lestat*, set in the city of New Orleans.

and Stan retired from San Francisco State University. In 1993 the family bought a former Catholic orphanage for girls, St. Elizabeth's.

In addition to her wildly popular vampire books, Rice wrote several novels about a circle of witches. *The Witching Hour* (1990) is about an evil spirit, Lasher. Other books in the series include *Lasher* (1993) and *Taltos* (1994). Although Rice does not believe in vampires, she thinks witches and ghosts might be possible. In 1999, Rice returned with another vampire story, *Vittorio, The Vampire.*

Rice continues to write very popular, and very scary, books. Her novels often take place in historical settings and rely on a great deal of careful research, which is unusual in the horror story tradition. Rice's recurring characters, especially the vampire Lestat, have a psychological complexity that allows them to grow and change as the stories progress. Like Stephen King, she is an international bestseller with a loyal and devoted following.

Stephen King
(1947–   )

For Stephen King, the real horror began on October 4, 1957.

It was on that day that ten year-old Stephen King sat in the movie theater in Stratford, Connecticut, watching a science-fiction film called *Earth vs. the Flying Saucers.*

Little Stephen King watched as outer-space aliens destroyed Washington, D.C. He was horrified as such landmarks as the Washington Monument and the capital building were destroyed by spaceships. That moment helped King see how potent are the things that really scare us, and what a personal feeling it is to be scared. Also, he realized that horror is an emotion that we struggle to overcome. "It [horror]

Stephen King

is a combat waged in the secret recesses of the heart," he later wrote.[1]

Stephen Edwin King was born on September 21, 1947, in Portland, Maine. He was the second son of Donald and Nellie Ruth King. In 1949, when Stephen was two years old, his father abandoned the family. Years later, when Stephen was twelve, he and his fourteen year-old brother David found a roll of film in the family attic. Putting what little money they had together, they rented a movie projector to watch the film. His father made the movies aboard a ship, and at one point the camera focuses on him. It was the only memory that King would have of his father.

David and Stephen King lived with their mother, who supported the family by working at a series of different jobs in Fort Wayne, Indiana and Stratford, Connecticut. Despite her best efforts, working as a doughnut-maker, store clerk and housekeeper, the family remained poor. In 1958, Nellie King and her children moved to Durham, Maine, to care for her aging parents.

"Those were very unhappy years for my mother," King recalls. "She had no money, she couldn't buy clothes, everything was handed down to her."[2]

When he was twelve or thirteen years old, King found a box of paperback books left behind by his father. Many of these books were horror stories by some of America's leading horror writers, including the American writer H. P. Lovecraft. Even though

King had previously enjoyed horror movies and comic books, these books, he wrote, were his "first encounter with serious fantasy-horror fiction,"[3] Soon the young man could often be found in the local library, reading classic American spooky stories.

He also spent his time writing. King knew that he wanted to be a writer at a very early age, and his first stories were fantasies or science-fiction. He wrote many stories that he sent to magazines, all of which were rejected. These early rejections didn't stop him from writing.

King began to publish his own work while attending high school in Lisbon Falls, Maine. One self-published story was a retelling of the movie version of Edgar Allan Poe's *The Pit and the Pendulum*. King made dozens of copies using his brother's printing press, and charged his classmates ten cents a copy. He sold almost all of them. Other self-made magazines include *People, Places, and Things—Volume I*, a 1963 collection of eighteen one-page horror and science fiction stories King created with his friend Chris Chesley, and *The Star Invaders*.

King started attending the University of Maine at Orono in 1966, where one of his teachers, Burton Hatlen, read and liked some of his stories. This show of support from one of his teachers helped give King confidence to continue writing and sending his stories to magazines. Before college, King had been published only in amateur magazines, or in his own, self-published books. But, in 1967, King sold his first story to a professional magazine, "The Glass Floor," published in *Startling Mystery Stories*, and he soon wrote his first novel, *The Long Walk*. He entered the book in a first-novel contest, but did not win. This discouraged him from sending the book to publishers. His second novel, also written during this period, *Sword in the Darkness*, was rejected by twelve publishers.

King's college years were productive and eventful. Aside from writing unpublished novels, he published many short stories, including "Night Surf" and "Stud City." More important, he met Tabitha Jane Spruce, who was studying English. Both worked in the school library, and they were married in 1971.

King also wrote a weekly column for the school newspaper, *The Maine Campus*. He was active in student politics and served as a member of the Student Senate, later criticizing the unpopular war between the United States and Vietnam.

King graduated from college with a degree in English. Upon leaving school, King was upset to learn that he could not easily find a job as a teacher or sell his work as a writer. He soon found work in an industrial laundry, where he earned sixty dollars a week. Tabitha also found it hard to find work as a writer or teacher after graduation, and she took a job as a waitress.

King was also frustrated by the lack of progress of his writing career. He worked at the laundry all day and wrote all night, completing a novel called *Getting*

It On early in 1971. An editor at Doubleday, a New York publishing house, was interested in the book, but the company turned it down. Fortunately, King was able to get a job that year as a teacher in Hampden Academy in Hampden, Maine.

The Kings and their first child, Naomi, born in 1971, moved into a trailer house in Hermon, Maine. He wrote in the furnace room of the trailer, typing his stories on an old typewriter balanced on top of a child's desk. He wrote another novel, *The Running Man*, during a single weekend. He could not sell this novel, either, and King feared he would never have a successful writing career. During this time the Kings had their second child, Joe, born in 1972, and the family lived in near poverty. Because of the pressure of work and family, King suffered "writer's block," a phrase writers use when stress or other problems keep them from writing.

While sitting in the furnace room of the trailer, King pulled an old, unpublished short story from his files and started to turn it into a novel. He did not like the progress he was making and threw the manuscript away. Tabitha pulled it out of the wastebasket and urged him to finish it. King thought the manuscript was "a certified loser,"[4] but he sent it to Doubleday anyway.

That book was *Carrie* (1974), and it became a bestseller. It was King's first published novel, and the money he earned from it let him leave teaching and write full time.

Carrie tells the story of high school student Carrie White, a shy girl with no friends. As Carrie grows older, she discovers that she has telekinesis, which is the ability to move things by thinking about them.

King based the character of Carrie on two girls he knew in high school. King made Carrie White believable to readers because he also wrote about her flaws and troubles. "The book tries to deal with the loneliness of one girl, her desperate effort to become part of the peer society in which she must exist, and how her effort fails," King said.[5]

King's next book is one of his most famous. *'Salem's Lot* (1975) tells the story of a small town in Maine that is taken over by vampires. Ben Mears, a writer who grew up in 'Salem's Lot and returns to write a book, teams up with high school student Mark Petrie to combat the vampires.

'Salem's Lot was one of the first American horror novels to update the vampire theme and place a supernatural story in a recognizable, small American town. The town of *'Salem's Lot* is very much like many real small towns in New England. *'Salem's Lot* established Stephen King as a great naturalist of horror fiction. His stories do not take place in far away remote and gloomy castles, but in towns and neighborhoods much like our own. The people in King's novels are not the mad scientists and evil aristocrats of earlier stories, but teachers, writers, doctors and high school kids.

Following the success of *'Salem's Lot*, King started producing books at a very fast rate. In the next few years he would write *The Shining* (1977), *The Stand* (1978), *The Dead Zone* (1979), *Firestarter* (1980), *Cujo* (1981), and many others.

King was not content to write only books. In 1982, he worked with a famous comic-book artist, Berni Wrightson, to create a giant-size comic-book called *Creepshow*. *Creepshow* is King's tribute to the horror comics he read while he grew up.

King finds ideas for stories everywhere. When King was a boy, he had a typewriter that was missing the "n" key. In the novel *Misery* (1987), Paul Sheldon wrote with this same old machine, missing "n" and all. When King's daughter Naomi's cat was accidentally killed, he came up with the plot of one of his most terrifying stories, *Pet Sematary* (1983).

Many of King's novels were turned into movies. *Carrie* was the first of King's novels turned into a successful film in 1976. *'Salem's Lot* became a four-hour television movie in 1979, and King himself directed *Maximum Overdrive* (1986). Kathy Bates won an Academy Award for her acting in the film version of King's *Misery* (1990). *Stand By Me* (1986), based on the short story "The Body" (1982), tells of four young boys who travel overnight along a railroad track to see the dead body of another boy who was hit by a train. During the trip, all of them grow up in some important way and learn the true meaning of friendship.

King writes so quickly that he adopted another name in 1977 to publish more books. The books that King published under the name Richard Bachman were often revised versions of novels he had written earlier. *Rage* (1977) was a revised version of *Getting It On*, first written eight years earlier. His novel *The Long Walk*, written during King's freshman year of college, was published under the Bachman name in 1979, and *The Running Man* was published in 1982.

In 1977, the Kings had a son, Owen. A dedicated family man, King coached his son's Little League team and later donated a one million dollar baseball stadium to his hometown of Bangor, Maine.[6] He writes in an office he built in his own home so that he can stay close to his family. King usually writes in the mornings, revising as he goes along, and attends to other business during the rest of the day. During the evening, he often listens to a local Bangor radio station, WZON, which he bought so it could play the variety of vintage rock-and-roll that he likes.

King's novels and short stories have won many awards, including the World Fantasy Award, the British Fantasy Award, and several Bram Stoker Awards (named after Bram Stoker, author of *Dracula*) from the Horror Writers Association.

Today, King lives in Maine with his wife, Tabitha, with frequent visits from their three grown children. King is the author of 33 novels, his latest being *Hearts in Atlantis*, in 1999, as well as dozens of short

The Stanley Hotel in Estes Park, Colorado. Stephen King used his own experience at the hotel as a setting in *The Shining*.

stories and several screenplays. He was hit by a car in the summer of 1999 and seriously injured, but soon made a recovery.[7] He has no plans to retire, and feels that writing is a way of staying young.

Writers, King says, are "paid to play, kind of like Michael Jordan and Mark McGwire. The rest of the generation grows up. We're left behind on the playground with the understanding that we will report on how it's going."[8]

Stephen King is one of the world's best known and most widely read living authors. He is the best-selling author of horror stories in history and is a major American cultural phenomenon. Many of his novels—notably *'Salem's Lot, Firestarter, Christine, It,* and *The Girl Who Loved Tom Gordon* (1999)—have young protagonists.

Chapter Notes

Chapter 1. Edgar Allan Poe

1. Daniel Hoffman, *Poe, Poe, Poe, Poe, Poe, Poe, Poe* (New York: Paragon House, 1972), p. 25.

2. Jeffrey Meyers, *Edgar Allan Poe: Life & Legacy* (New York: Macmillan Library Reference, 1992), p. 89.

3. Ibid., p. 44.

4. Chris Steinbrunner and Otto Penzler, eds., *The Encyclopedia of Mystery and Detection* (San Diego, California: McGraw-Hill Books, 1976), p. 311.

5. Stephen Peithman, ed., *The Annotated Tales of Edgar Allan Poe* (New York: Crown Publishers, 1986), p. xii.

6. N. P. Willis, *The Death of Edgar A. Poe* (New York: World Syndicate Publishing Company, 1920), p. 30.

Chapter 2. Ambrose Bierce

1. Jack Sullivan, ed., "Ambrose Bierce (1842–1914)," *The Penguin Encyclopedia of Horror and the Supernatural* (New York: Viking Penguin, 1986), p. 33.

2. Roy Morris Jr., *Ambrose Bierce: Alone in Bad Company* (New York: Crown Publishers, 1996), p. 79.

3. Petri Liukkonen, "Ambrose Bierce," Courtesy of Pegasos-Literature related resources, <http://www.kirjasto.sci.fi/bierce.htm> (August, 17, 2000).

4. Ibid.

5. H. P. Lovecraft, *Supernatural Horror in Literature* (Mineola, New York: Dover Books, 1973), p. 67.

6. Morris, p. 158.

Chapter 3. H. P. Lovecraft

1. S.T. Joshi, "Howard Phillips Lovecraft: The Life of a Gentleman of Providence," The H. P. Lovecraft Archive, March 30, 1999, <http://www.hplovecraft.com/life/biograph.htm> (August, 17, 2000).

2. Letter from Lovecraft to R. H. Barlow, April 10, 1934.

3. Joshi.

4. Walter Kendrick, *The Thrill of Fear: Two-Hundred & Fifty Years of Scary Entertainment* (New York: Grove Atlantic, 1991), p. 196–197.

5. L. Sprague de Camp, *H .P. Lovecraft: A Biography* (Lanham, Maryland: Barnes & Noble Books, 1996), p. 256–257.

6. Ibid., p. 428.

Chapter 4. Robert Bloch

1. Robert Bloch, *Once Around the Bloch: An Unauthorized Autobiography* (New York: Tor Books, 1993), p. 45.

2. Ibid., p. 47.

3. Ibid., p. 71.

4. Stephen King, *Danse Macabre*, Rev. ed., (New York: Berkley Books, 1982), p. 75–77.

5. Walter Kendrick, *The Thrill of Fear: Two-Hundred & Fifty Years of Scary Entertainment* (New York: Grove Atlantic, 1991), p. 231.

Chapter 5. Shirley Jackson

1. Lenemaja Friedman, *Shirley Jackson* (Boston: Twayne Publishers, 1975), pp. 17–18.

2. Ibid., pp. 20–21.

3. Ibid., pp. 21–26.

4. Judy Oppenheimer, *Private Demons: The Life of Shirley Jackson* (New York: G.P. Putnam's Sons, 1988), pp. 128–130.

5. Ibid. p.60

6. Ibid., p. 226–227, 242.

7. Friedman, p. 36.

Chapter 6. Rod Serling

1. Joel Engel, *Rod Serling: The Dreams and Nightmare of Life in the Twilight Zone* (Lincolnwood, Il.: Contemporary Books, 1989), p. 1.

2. Marc Scott Zicree, *The Twilight Zone Companion* (New York: Bantam Books, 1982), p. 23.

3. Engel, p. 57.

4. Gordon F. Sander, *The Rise and Twilight of Television's Last Angry Man* (New York: Dutton Plume, 1992), p. 61.

5. Ed Naha, "Rod Serling's Dream," *Starlog Magazine*, August 1978, p. 36.

6. Ibid.

7. Engel, p.170.

8. Naha, p. 39.

9. Linda Brevelle, "Rod Serling's Last Interview," *Writer's Yearbook* (1976), p. 104.

Chapter 7. Dean Koontz

1. David Robinson and Dean Koontz, *Beautiful Death: The Art of the Cemetery* (New York: Penguin Studio, 1996), p. 6.

2. Martin H. Greenberg, Ed Gorman and Bill Munster eds., *The Dean Koontz Companion* (New York: Berkley Books, 1994), pp. 10–11.

3. Ibid., p. 10.

4. Ibid., pp. 19–20, 23, 290, 302, 304.

5. Robinson and Koontz, pp. 6–7.

6. Douglas Winter, "Writers of Today," Jack Sullivan, ed., *The Penguin Encyclopedia of Horror and the Supernatural* (Viking Penguin, 1986), pp. 468–474.

7. Greenberg, p. 53.

Chapter 8. R. L. Stine

1. R. L. Stine, as told to Joe Arthur, *It Came From Ohio! My Life as a Writer* (New York: Scholastic, 1997), pp. 13–17.

2. Ibid., p. 28.

3. Ibid., pp. 44–47.

4. "A Chat With R. L. Stine," *Scholastic Network*, October 31, 1994, <http://www.scholastic.com/Goosebumps/low/stine/chat.htm> (August 18, 2000).

5. Maurice Horn, ed., *The World Encyclopedia of Comics*, (Avon, 1976), p. 273.

6. Stine, *It Came From Ohio*, p. 55.

Chapter 9. Anne Rice

1. Katherine Ramsland, *Prism of the Night: A Biography of Anne Rice* (New York: Plume/Penguin, 1992), p. 2.

2. Ibid., p. 46.

3. Michael Riley, *Conversations With Anne Rice* (New York: Plume/Penguin, 1996), p. 73.

4. Matthew Bunson, *The Vampire Encyclopedia* (New York: Crown Publishers, 1993), p. 134.

5. David J. Skal, *V is for Vampire: The A-Z Guide to Everything Undead* (New York: Plume/Penguin, 1995), pp. 172–174.

Chapter 10. Stephen King

1. Stephen King, *Danse Macabre*, Rev. ed. (New York: Berkley Books, 1982), p.12.

2. Mark Singer, "What Are You Afraid Of?" *The New Yorker*, September 7, 1998, p. 61.

3. King, p. 96.

4. Douglas E. Winter, *Art of Darkness: Life & Fiction of the Master of the Macabre, Stephen King* (Signet Books, 1986), pp. 28–29.

5. Ibid., p. 33.

6. Bob Minzesheimer, "Horror's Home Run King," *USA Today*, September 17, 1998, p. D1.

7. John Morgan and Dr. Stephen A. Shoop, "Stephen King Fights Back From 'Dead Zone,'" *USA Today Health*, February 2, 2000.

8. Minzesheimer, "Horror's Home Run King."

Further Reading and Selected Bibliography
(with Internet Addresses)

A Selected List

Bunson, Matthew. *The Vampire Encyclopedia*. New York: Crown Publishing Group, 1993.

Kendrick, Walter. *The Thrill of Fear: 250 Years of Scary Entertainment*. New York: Grove Atlantic, Inc. 1993.

Sullivan, Jack. *The Penguin Encyclopedia of Horror*. New York: Viking Penguin, 1999.

The date in parenthesis is the year the work was published.

Edgar Allan Poe:

<http://dcls.org/x/archives/poe.html>

<http://bau2.uibk.ac.at/sg/poe/Bio.html>

Tamerlane and Other Poems (1827)

El Araaf, Tamerlane, and Minor Poems (1829)

Tales of the Grotesque and Arabesque (1840)

Tales of Edgar Allan Poe (1845)

The Raven and Other Poems (1845)

Ambrose Bierce:

<http://sunsite.berkeley.edu/Literature/Bierce>

Tales of Soldiers and Civilians (1891)

Can Such Things Be? (1893)

The Collected Works of Ambrose Bierce (1909)

Ghost and Horror Stories of Ambrose Bierce (1964)

A Vision of Doom (1980)

H. P. Lovecraft:

<http://horrorbooks.about.com/arts/horrorbooks.about.com/ ars/horrorbook/gi/dynamic/offsite.htm>

<http://www.hplovecraft.com>

The Shadow Over Innsmouth (1936)

The Outsider and Others (1939)

Beyond the Wall of Sleep (1943)

Marginalia (1944)

At the Mountains of Madness (1964)

Dagon and Other Macabre Tales (1965)

Robert Bloch:

Bloch, Robert. *Once Around the Bloch: An Unauthorized Autobiography.* New York: Tor Books, 1993.

<http://www.kirjasto.sci.fi/rbloch.htm>

Sea-Kissed (1945)

The Opener of the Way (1945)

The Scarf (1947)

The Kidnapper (1954)

The Will to Kill (1954)

Psycho (1959)

The Deadbeat (1960)

Pleasant Dreams (1960)

Ladies Day (1968)

This Crowded Earth (1968)

Night-World (1972)

American Gothic (1974)

Strange Eons (1978)

Psycho II (1982)

Night of the Ripper (1984)

Lori (1989)

Psycho House (1990)

Once Around the Bloch (1993)

Shirley Jackson:

<http://home.rochester.rr.com/biffio/ed/eklor.html>

<http://underthesun.cc/Classics/Jackson/shirley_jackson.htm>

The Lottery, or The Adventures of James Harris (1949)

Hangsaman (1950)

The Sundial (1958)

The Haunting of Hill House (1959)

We Have Always Lived in the Castle (1962)

The Magic of Shirley Jackson (1966)

Come Along with Me (1968)

Rod Serling:

Zicree, Marc S. *The Twilight Zone Companion*. New York: Bantam Books, 1989.

<http://rodserling.com>

<http://www.scifi.com/twizone/twilight5.html>

Playhouse 90 (Screenplays)

Twilight Zone (92 episodes)

Rod Serling's Night Gallery

Dean Koontz:

<http://horrorbooks.about.com/arts/horrorbooks/cs/
deankoontz/index.htm

Anti-Man (1970)

Blood Risk (1973)

Demon Seed (1973)

Whispers (1980)

Phantoms (1983)

Darkfall (1984)

Watchers (1987)

Lightning (1988)

Oddkins (1988)

Midnight (1989)

The Bad Place (1990)

Cold Fire (1991)

Hideaway (1992)

Mr. Murder (1993)

Dragon Tears (1993)

Winter Moon (1994)

Seize the Night (1999)

R. L. Stine:

Stine, R. L. *It Came From Ohio!: My Life As a Writer.* New
York: Scholastic Inc., 1997

<http://www.scholastic.com/Goosebumps/low/stine/index.htm>

The *Fear Street* series including

Silent Night

Switched

Welcome to Dead House
Say Cheese
The *Goosebumps* series including
Night of the Living Dummy
Stay out of the Basement
The Haunted Mask

Anne Rice:

<http://www.annerice.com>
Interview with the Vampire (1976)
The Feast of All Saints (1979)
The Vampire Lestat (1985)
The Queen of the Damned (1988)
The Mummy (1989)
The Witching Hour (1990)
The Tale of the Body Thief (1992)
Lasher (1993)
Taltos (1994)
Memnoch the Devil (1995)
Servant of the Bones (1996)
Vittorio, The Vampire (1999)

Stephen King:

Wilson, Suzan. *Stephen King: King of Thrillers and Horror.* Berkeley Heights, NJ: Enslow Publishers, Inc., 2000.

<http://www.stephenking.com>

<http://www.stephenkingnews.com/>

Carrie (1974)

'Salem's Lot (1975)

The Shining (1977)

Night Shift (1978)

The Stand (1978)

The Dead Zone (1979)

Firestarter (1980)

Danse Macabre (1981)

Cujo (1981)

Different Seasons (1982)

Creepshow (1982)

Christine (1983)

Pet Sematary (1983)

The Talisman (1984)

Misery (1987)

The Tommyknockers (1987)

The Dark Half (1989)

Needful Things (1991)

Gerald's Game (1992)

Dolores Claiborne (1992)

Nightmares & Dreamscapes (1993)

Insomnia (1994)

Rose Madder (1995)

The Green Mile (1996)

Desperation (1996)

Bag of Bones (1998)

The Girl Who Loved Tom Gordon (1999)

Hearts in Atlantis (1999)

Index